A New View

Dissociative Identity Disorder (In Pictures)

Kate Thompson – Deep Waters

TRAPPED INSIDE, UNTIL ONE DAY THE BARS COME DOWN.

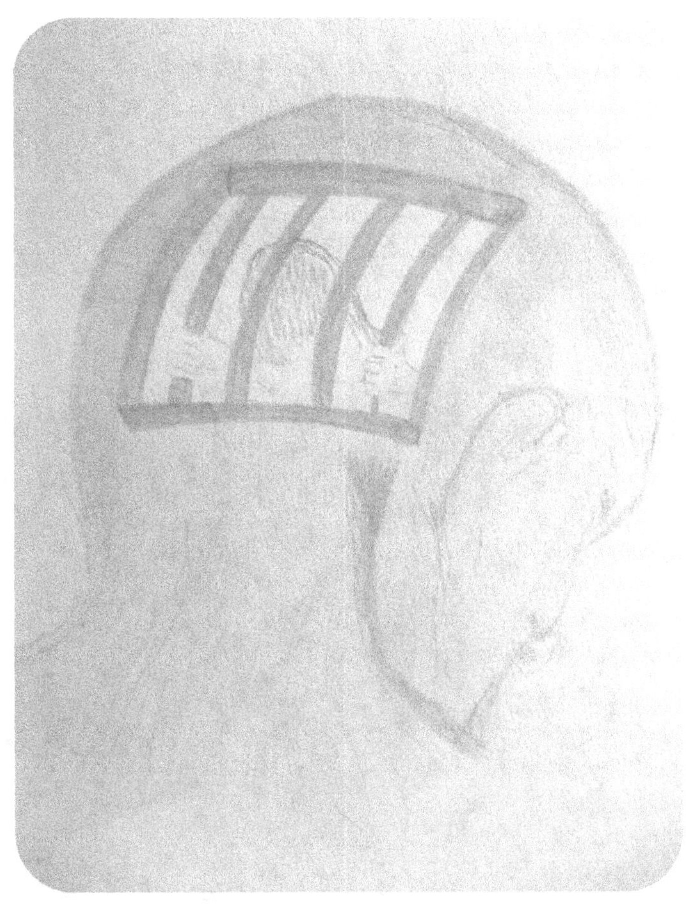

LOOKING FROM THE INSIDE,
I SEE THE OUTSIDE WORLD.

I HOLD ONTO THE SAFETY OF WHAT I KNOW.

I CANNOT SPEAK. I WAS
TAUGHT WELL,   THEY SAY
I'M 34,   BUT I'M NOT,   I'M
3.

© K.Thopmson

WE ARE NOT ALL SMALL;
SOME OF US REMEMBER
DIFFERENT TIMES IN OUR
LIFE.

I'M PEERING OUT THROUGH THE CRACKS INTO A WORLD I JUST DON'T UNDERSTAND. THIS IS NOT THE SAME WORLD I ONCE LIVED IN. HERE, I WATCH ASKING THE QUESTION "IS IT SAFE TO COME OUT?"

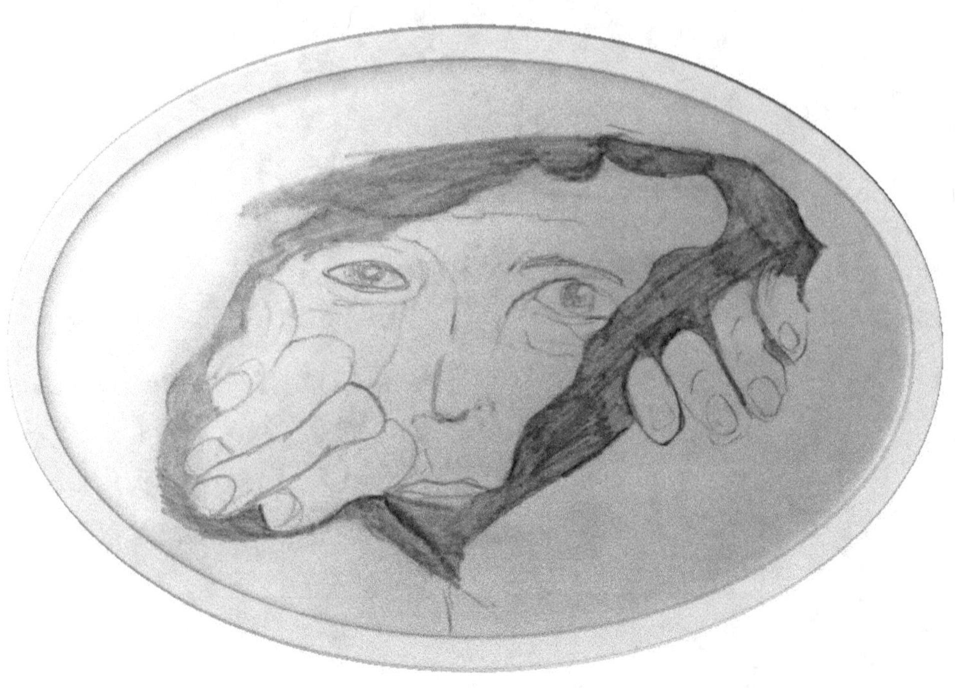

WHO AM I? WHO ARE WE?
THE MANY
INSIDE
REPRESENT ALL
OF ME.

SOME OF US LOOK A LITTLE DIFFERENT TO EACH OTHER. SOME HAVE DIFFERENT NAMES. SOME OF US ARE GIRLS, SOME ARE BOYS.

SOME OF US ARE HAPPY
AND SOME ARE NOT. SOME
OF US SELF- HARM SOME
DON'T. WE ALL DO WHAT
WE CAN TO TRY AND
COPE.

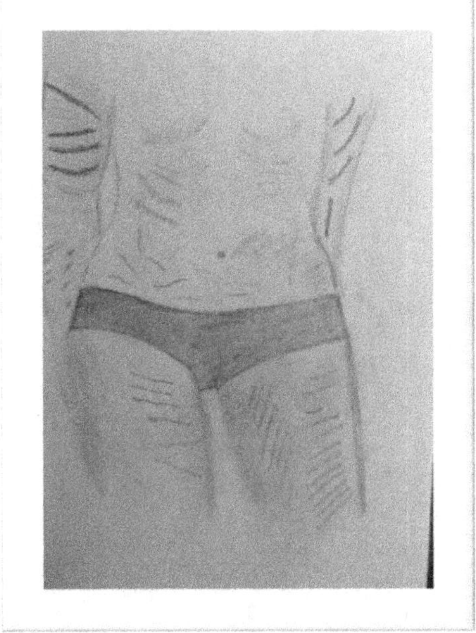

IT'S NOT ALL BAD
THOUGH,
SOME OF US
HAVE GOOD
FUN.

ONCE WE GET TO KNOW EACH OTHER, WE CAN PLAY TOGETHER AND TALK TO EACH OTHER.

JUST LIKE MEETING ANYONE NEW, IT CAN TAKE A WHILE TO GET TO KNOW EACH OTHER.

IF WE ALL WORK AT IT,
WE CAN LEARN TO LIVE
AS ONE FAMILY. LISTEN AND
HELP EACH OTHER, PLAY
AND HAVE FUN TOGETHER.

SOMETIMES WE HAVE TO HEAR THE CRIES OF THE OTHERS INSIDE.

THE FEARS AND HURTS
WITHIN US ARE OFTEN
HARD TO GET TO. WE
HAVE MANY DEFENCE
SYSTEMS IN PLACE,   TO
STOP THE HURTING.

IT MAY SEEM STRANGE, BUT WHY WOULD WE WANT TO REMEMBER THE BAD THINGS THAT HAVE HAPPENED TO US?

EVENTUALLY WE HAVE TO,
AND THEN, WE OFTEN
NEED HELP.

IT MAY START WITH ONE
OF US, BUT
COULD END
UP WITH
MANY.

THE TRAUMA ONCE OUT OF
THE BOX CAN CAUSE MANY
DISRUPTIONS.

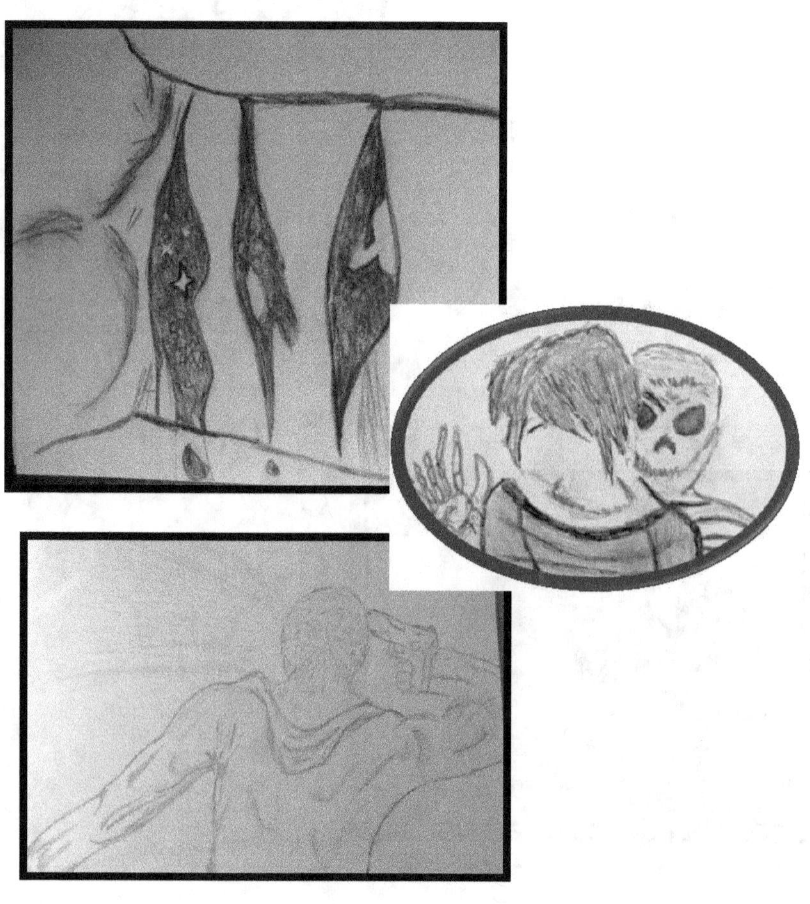

OUR BROKENNESS AND NEED WILL BE ON SHOW. THAT MIGHT BE SCARY FOR YOU, BUT IT WILL BE FOR US TOO.

STICK WITH US, THE INNER CRIES WILL COME TO THE SURFACE. HEALING WILL HAPPEN. JUST GIVE US TIME.

SO D.I.D FOR ME IS WHO I
AM; WHO WE ARE! WE
ARE MANY.

WE WEAR MASKS AND
HAVE HURTS AND FEARS
TOO, JUST LIKE YOU.

WE CAN HEAL AND LIVE
AGAIN; MAYBE YOU CAN
HELP US ON THAT JOURNEY?